SEEK & FIND UNICORNS

BY SIMON ABBOTT

PETER PAUPER PRESS, INC.
White Plains, New York

PETER PAUPER PRESS
Fine Books and Gifts Since 1928

Our Company

In 1928, at the age of twenty-two, Peter Beilenson began print-ing books on a small press in the basement of his parents' home in Larchmont, New York. Peter—and later, his wife, Edna—sought to create fine books that sold at "prices even a pauper could afford."

Today, still family owned and operated, Peter Pauper Press con-tinues to honor our founders' legacy of quality, value, and fun for big kids and small kids alike.

For Dora and Tabby...
happy searching!

Illustrations copyright © 2020 Simon Abbott
Designed by Heather Zschock

Copyright © 2020
Peter Pauper Press, Inc.
Manufactured for Peter Pauper Press, Inc.
202 Mamaroneck Avenue
White Plains, NY 10601 USA

ISBN 978-1-4413-3502-9

Printed in China

Published in the United Kingdom and Europe by
Peter Pauper Press, Inc., c/o White Pebble International
Unit 2, Plot 11 Terminus Road
Chichester, West Sussex PO19 8TX, UK

Library of Congress Cataloging-in-Publication Data Available

Printed in China

7 6 5 4 3 2 1

Visit us at www.peterpauper.com

Did you know that unicorns' favorite game is hide and seek?

A whole herd of fun-loving unicorns have hidden themselves in the pages ahead, and it's up to you to find them!

You'll probably see some of them right away, and have to search long and hard to track down others. On the left side of each scene are pictures of all the unicorns you're looking for in that scene! Can you find them all?

If you're up for some extra sleuthing, on the right side of each scene are other hidden things to look for.

Get ready for a magical challenge!

Unicorns
to find:

Other things to find:

Unicorns
to find:

Other things to find:

Unicorns
to find:

Other things to find:

Unicorns to find:

Unicorns
to find:

Other things to find:

Unicorns to find:

Unicorns
to find:

Unicorns to find:

Other things
to find:

Unicorns to find:

Other things to find:

Unicorns
to find:

Other things
to find:

Unicorns
to find:

Other things
to find:

Unicorns
to find:

Other things
to find:

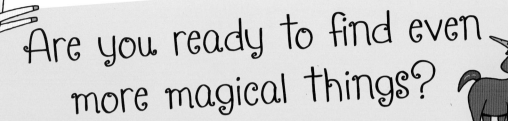

Are you ready to find even more magical things?

A chocolate ice cream cone, a blue and white striped pail, a yellow tutu, a purple pair of pants, a scarecrow, an apple tree, two lion cubs, four giraffes, an orange alien in a green spacecraft, a pink and red spotted planet, a crab, a white pearl necklace, a rainbow, a stagecoach, a helicopter, a cat in a window, a fox, a plate with two cupcakes, a pink pair of boots, a cactus in a pot, a teddy bear in a window, a green and red hot air balloon, a snowman with a purple hat, and a Christmas wreath. This is tricky... sometimes there are more than one!

Now, discover some on your own!